THE LIT
HOUS
TIPS

WILLIAM FORTT

THE LITTLE BOOK OF HOUSEPLANT TIPS

WILLIAM FORTT

Absolute Press

First published in Great Britain in 2008 by
Absolute Press
Scarborough House, 29 James Street West
Bath BA1 2BT, England
Phone 44 (0) 1225 316013 **Fax** 44 (0) 1225 445836
E-mail info@absolutepress.co.uk
Web www.absolutepress.co.uk

A catalogue record of this book is available from the British Library

ISBN 13: 9781904573951

Printed and bound in China by 1010

‘It shot up like a rocket till it nearly touched the sky. It’s the biggest aspidistra in the world’.

Will E. Haines, Jimmy Harper and Tommy Connor, 1928

1

Houseplants

are different. Ordinary outdoor plants survive all kinds of indignities, including neglect and unsuitable locations. Nature looks after them. But indoor plants are in an unnatural environment.

To stay alive and healthy, they **need considerate handling and regular attention.**

2

Think carefully before you buy a houseplant.

What are its special requirements? Full sun? Partial shade? High humidity? Moderate temperatures? Shelter from draughts? Suit your purchases to the conditions your home can provide.

3

Get to know the broad categories of houseplants.

The major division is between flowering plants and foliage plants. Within these are: trailers and climbers (such as the ivies), palms, cacti and species which produce plantlets (such as the spider plant).

4

Keep your house as dust-free as possible.

Dust particles can harm houseplants by settling on the leaves and clogging the pores. Once a week, clean the leaves gently with cotton wool soaked in tepid water (but spare newly-formed leaves until they've toughened up a bit).

5

Bear in mind

what height and shape your houseplant will eventually reach. Will it grow tall and straight? Will it bush out and demand more sideways space? Is there enough room for trailing tendrils or aerial roots? Where will you put it when it's fully developed?

6

Select the right plant for each part of the house, because different areas will give different conditions. South- and west-facing rooms give the most light, whereas east- and north-facing ones will be darker. A hallway or lobby will be cooler than a sitting room. Bathrooms and kitchens are likely to be humid. And so on.

7

Use houseplants to clean the air in your home!

NASA scientists have shown (yes, really) that they can filter out common household pollutants such as ammonia and benzene. On top of that, many houseplants release chemicals which suppress airborne microbes and molds.

8

Basic houseplant needs #1: light.

Plants live by photosynthesis, harnessing the energy of light to produce their food. So most have to get at least twelve hours of light to stimulate flowering (though the needs of individual plants vary widely).

9

Central heating makes the air in your home very dry – too dry for the health of many plants. It is vital to re-humidify the atmosphere at a consistent rate. Put shallow trays of water near the plants, or put the pot inside a bigger one, filling the gap between with dampened peat.

10

Natural light or artificial?

Sunlight is best, of course, but this will vary hugely according to the season or the siting of your windows. In some cases, some artificial light will help plants along. Use fluorescent bulbs rather than ordinary incandescent ones, as they are better for encouraging foliage growth.

11

Keep plants away from extremes of light or heat.

If they are too close to windows, they may suffer from excesses of heat and cold, as well as bright sunlight. Likewise those near radiators, wood stoves or air-conditioning vents may get too hot or too cold.

12

Where's **the best place to buy houseplants?**

Certainly a proper **nursery or garden centre** are the most reliable sources. Make sure the plants are clearly labelled. Also check that they are well looked after, and displayed indoors or under sheltered conditions in cold weather.

13

How to spot a healthy houseplant.

The leaves should be evenly spaced and vibrant, with no browning or curling. The stems should be firm and sturdy. The flowers should be bright and well-coloured. Look at the bottom of the pot to make sure roots aren't poking out – a sign of being pot-bound.

14

Remember that stems and leaves will grow towards the source of light.

If this is fixed (such as a lamp or a window), the plant will soon look weirdly lopsided. Turn it 180 degrees every few days so that it grows evenly.

15

Houseplants are part of your home's décor, so **display them to their best advantage.** Some large or bold plants look good on their own. Others can be grouped together to create interesting shapes and varying shades. Make use of contrasts – in leaf sizes and textures, or in flower colour.

16

Pots and other containers can transform a houseplant display. Ordinary clay or plastic flowerpots are fine, but experiment with bolder shapes and materials. Mix tall and squat containers, or similar shapes in different sizes. And find colours which enhance (not copy) the shades of flowers and foliage.

17

Some plants look better together. Two or three begonias in one container, for example, can give a more striking impression than a singleton. The same goes for varieties of sansevieria, zebra plant and prayer plant – in fact most species with large variegated leaves.

18

Basic houseplant needs #2: water.

Water has two major jobs. It gives strength, which keeps the plant rigid and upright. And it absorbs nutrients from the soil or compost and transports them via the leaves and roots. Deprived of rainfall, houseplants depend on you for their water supply.

19

Train climbing plants with aerial roots up a moss pole.

Either wrap some sphagnum moss round a wooden stake and bind with wire, or make a tube with chicken wire and stuff it with moss. In either case, it should be about 90cm (3ft) high and firmly fixed in the pot. Tie the roots to the pole with string.

20

Give your plants just enough water.

Too much will clog up the compost in the pot and prevent the roots from getting enough oxygen. In winter, it can also cool the plant fatally. Make sure you know how much each plant needs, and stick to that quantity.

21

If possible, use rainwater for watering plants. Otherwise, tap water is OK, as long as you let it stand for an hour or two before applying. This brings it up to room temperature and gives the chlorine time to dissipate. The best bet is to fill up watering cans the night before using them.

22

Water your plants mainly from below

rather than on top. Make sure your pots stand in saucers, which can easily be filled with water. Submerge badly dried-out pots in a bucket of water. When the bubbles stop, lift out the pot and allow to drain before restoring to its saucer.

23

It's best to

use a sharp pair of scissors

when **cutting, pruning or tidying up**

your houseplants. Blunt scissors, or a less than razor-sharp knife, can easily damage the stems by tearing or bruising. Disease spores will soon get to work.

24

Plants in strong sunlight will suffer if you splash water on the leaves.

A water droplet acts like a magnifying glass, concentrating the sun's heat and scorching the leaf. Water these plants very carefully to avoid wetting the foliage.

25

Which houseplants are easiest to grow?

Good beginner's plants tend to have homely names like parlour palm, mother-in-law's tongue, rubber plant and piggy-back plant. These, along with old favourites like common ivy, spider plant and false castor oil plant (*fatsia japonica*) are tough enough to survive a few mistakes.

26

Basic houseplant needs #3: food.

During their active growing season, plants require regular feeding with mineral nutrients. These are vital for growth and general health. They can be incorporated in the compost, or you can add them in liquid or solid form.

27

Give climbers something to cling onto. Vines, ivies, philodendrons and other climbing plants can be trained up frames of bamboo or plastic, firmly pushed into the soil. Attach the stems loosely to the frames with twine or soft wire.

28

Most houseplants need

occasional pruning and tidying up.

Clear away dead foliage and 'deadhead' old flowers between finger and thumb. Prune with secateurs or scissors in the spring to get rid of overlong stems and tangled growth. Always cut just above a bud, and angled away from it.

29

Grow a lemon tree from a pip.

Press 6 lemon pips into a pot filled with seed compost (just below the surface). Water, cover with a plastic bag and leave in a warm place. Within a few weeks, you'll see shoots: remove the bag. Once plants are big enough, pot them out singly. You'll get flowers but no lemons, sadly.

30

A bathroom is the perfect spot for plants which need high humidity.

These include species from tropical regions, such as maidenhair fern, wax plant, creeping fig and African violets. They will suffer, though, from dramatic drops in temperature (usually caused by leaving windows open in winter).

31

Most houseplants enjoy a humidity level of about 60 per cent.

You can help by spraying leaves with water from a fine mist sprayer. Or place pots in a tray of pebbles or gravel which are kept moist. The water will evaporate steadily.

32

What about those pokey, draughty, dark corners?

Yes, there are even houseplants which like these. The legendary aspidistra will survive here happily, along with ivies, fatsias (false castor oil plant) and some varieties of philodendron.

33

Watch out for pot-bound plants. These have grown too big for their pots. They fail to thrive and dry out quickly. It's time to move them to bigger premises. Tip out the plant carefully and crumble away some of the old, worn-out soil. Then **pop it into a larger pot** and fill up carefully with new compost. Water in well.

34

Basic houseplant needs #4: warmth. Quite a few common houseplants originate from tropical or sub tropical parts of the world, so they require temperatures somewhere between 15–21°C to thrive in. They intensely dislike big drops in temperature, which usually occur at night.

35

After a plant has finished **its annual growing phase,** it needs a rest. **Move it to a cooler part of the house** while it is dormant. At the same time, cut down its water supply. Then it shows signs of growth again, move it back to a warmer room.

36

Remember: **warmth is only one part of the equation.**

If you give a houseplant more heat, it will grow faster. It will therefore need

more light

to produce more food. At the same time, the heat will dry out the air, so

more water

is needed to create humidity.

37

Buy a bromeliad.

These extraordinary tropical plants (most of which grow on trees) are daunting but rewarding. They need special bromeliad compost mixture and special feeds once a month. You must also fill the central 'urn' of the plant with fresh water each month. They do well in a warm bathroom.

38

Enjoy hyacinths and tulips at Christmas. At the start of autumn, plant specially prepared bulbs in seed compost or bulb fibre (you can put several in one bowl). Keep in a dark place and after about two months shoots will appear. Move the pots – first to a shaded room, then to a brighter spot in time for the festivities.

39

Create your own piece of desert, with a cactus garden.

Put a layer of gravel, then one of a sandy compost mixture, into a wide, shallow pot. Plant out a variety of desert cacti. Water very lightly and keep in a sunny place. And remember – cacti are naturally happy with low humidity.

40

Going away on holiday?

Ask a competent neighbour to tend your houseplants. Failing that,

prepare rigorously.

Pick off old foliage and flowers, then group the plants all together. Set up some capillary matting or put the plants in shallow trays with water. Water thoroughly before you go. Shut the door firmly.

41

Watch out for insect pests. Hordes of them penetrate the great indoors, and **many are hard to spot.** Be alert for tiny red dots (red spider mites), anything which looks like a small woodlouse (mealy bugs), and tiddly flies which are white, green or black. Zap them all with derris dust.

42

Remove all sickly-looking leaves and flowers at once. Diseases spread fast between plants, causing black and white moulds, rotting slimy stems and other horrors. Try soapy water for the moulds. Rotten stems should be cut off: in serious cases the whole plant will have to go.

43

Pests can be surprisingly large. Among the bigger blighters that find their way in (especially to conservatories) are slugs, snails and caterpillars. Pick them off and send them packing or they can do a lot of damage very quickly. Even the admirable earthworm can be a nuisance indoors.

44

Divide and multiply. You can easily increase your stock of ferns, African violets and other multi-stemmed plants by dividing them. Tip the plant gently from its pot,

then tease apart the roots

so you end up with two or three separate bunches. Plant each in a pot with medium potting compost.

45

Plants with variegated leaves sometimes produce solid green shoots (this can be encouraged by overfeeding). Remove them at once, because they will develop faster than their multi-shaded rivals. In time, they'll take over and your plant will be variegated no more.

46

Give your houseplants a breath of fresh air. Stand them outside on a warm and still summer's day, preferably in a gentle drizzle. This will perk them up no end, washing off dust, and giving outdoor predators a chance to pick off insect pests.

47

How do you take a cactus out of its pot?

The answer is: with care. Fold a sheet of newspaper into a suitably-sized strip. Wrap it carefully round the cactus, leaving enough at either end to grip onto. With your other hand, pull away the pot. The cactus is now ready for re-potting.

48

Buy a maximum-and-minimum thermometer.

You may think you know the temperature in your own home, but it's best to have an accurate reading. Hang the thermometer in different rooms of the house, and you'll soon see the temperature highs and lows throughout the day.

49

New plants from old: take leaf cuttings.

In late summer, cut a few healthy leaves (with stalks) from fleshy-leaved plants such as begonia and African violet. Dip the ends in hormone rooting powder and put into a pot filled with cuttings compost. Water and pop a plastic bag on top. Roots should show in about a month.

50

Some plants

are potted up especially to

flower indoors in early spring.

These include azaleas, chrysanthemums, geraniums and some begonias. When they have finished flowering, plant them in a sheltered spot out in the garden, or in the greenhouse.

William Fortt

William Fortt is a gardener of long standing, whose cottage garden in Wiltshire, is famed for the beauty of its rare plants and the wonders of its many varieties of culinary and medicinal herbs. He has been an author for more than 30 years, with many books to his name.

THE LITTLE BOOK OF

TIPS SERIES

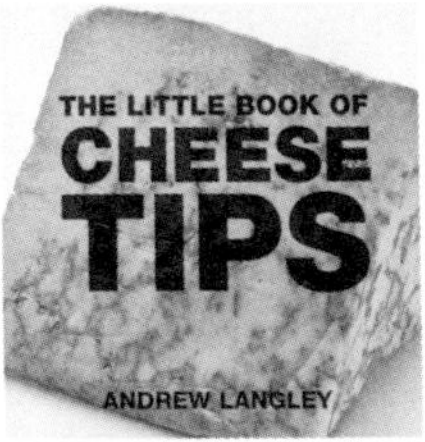
THE LITTLE BOOK OF
CHEESE
TIPS
ANDREW LANGLEY

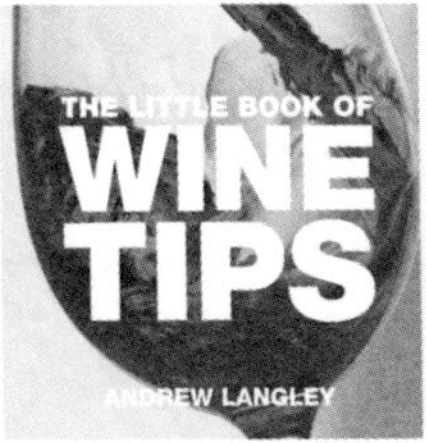
THE LITTLE BOOK OF
WINE
TIPS
ANDREW LANGLEY

THE LITTLE BOOK OF
AGA
TIPS 2
RICHARD MAGGS

THE LITTLE BOOK OF
COFFEE
TIPS
ANDREW LANGLEY

THE LITTLE BOOK OF
TEA
TIPS
ANDREW LANGLEY

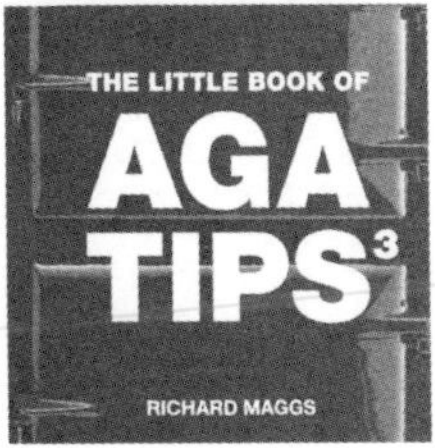
THE LITTLE BOOK OF
AGA
TIPS 3
RICHARD MAGGS

THE LITTLE BOOK OF
AGA
TIPS
RICHARD MAGGS

THE LITTLE BOOK OF
CHRISTMAS
AGA
TIPS
RICHARD MAGGS

THE LITTLE BOOK OF
RAYBURN
TIPS
RICHARD MAGGS

THE LITTLE BOOK OF
BRIDGE
TIPS
CHRIS JONES

THE LITTLE BOOK OF
CHESS
TIPS
PETER FRENCH

THE LITTLE BOOK OF
FISHING
TIPS
MICK DEVENISH

THE LITTLE BOOK OF
GREEN
TIPS
WILLIAM FORTT

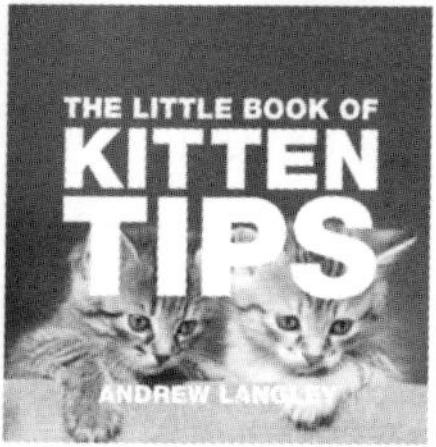
THE LITTLE BOOK OF
KITTEN
TIPS
ANDREW LANGLEY

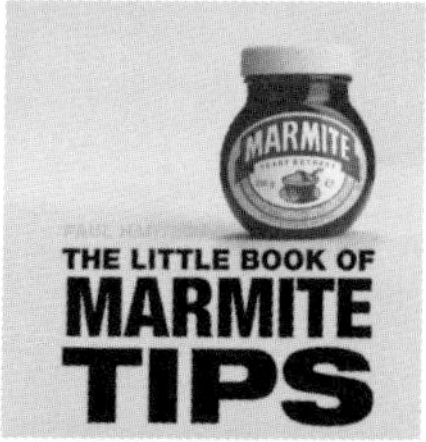
MARMITE
THE LITTLE BOOK OF
MARMITE
TIPS

THE LITTLE BOOK OF
PUPPY
TIPS
ANDREW LANGLEY

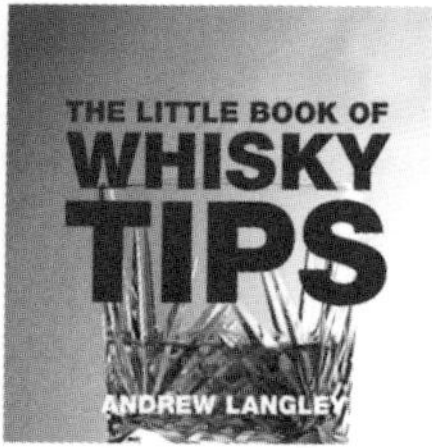
THE LITTLE BOOK OF
WHISKY
TIPS
ANDREW LANGLEY

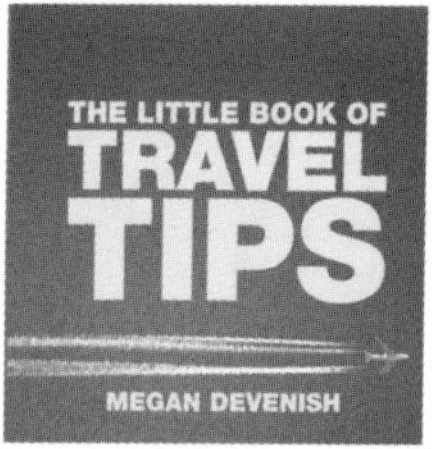
THE LITTLE BOOK OF
TRAVEL
TIPS
MEGAN DEVENISH